Age of Unrest

Jordan Bartley

Presentation by *BookLeaf Publishing*

Web: www.bookleafpub.com

E-mail: info@bookleafpub.com

ISBN: 9789357444354

First edition 2022

DEDICATION

Abundance of gratitude to the entrusted few in my circle. Your support kept me going when I wanted to surrender.

PREFACE

Upon turning 31, I had high hopes for the future and the promises that year would bring. Within the first three months there has been trauma, heart ache and sorrow. It's scary to put yourself out there. To be so exposed to the people around you. Yet, here I am, exploring deep within myself to navigate through this period in life.

Currently, Me

Brain filled with running thoughts
Relationships, work, insecurities.
Emotions at an all-time high
Anger, sadness, fear.
Mental health in a downward spiral
Depression, anxiety, insomnia.
Physical symptoms manifesting from stress
Fatigue, nausea, migraines.
Imbalance of spirit by overwhelming worry
Ungrounded, lacking faith, disconnected.

More Than A Virus

I went home sick from work
Feels like a cold with body aches
Little bit of a cough, runny nose
Nope, it's not Covid.

I have been home sick for two days
Must be the flu, because I am not improving
Lost my sense of smell and taste, but that is just
my stuffed up nose
Please, don't be Covid.

I have been home sick for five days
This is not good; I cannot eat or stay awake
Fever is high, symptoms increasing, time to take
a test
Positive, I have Covid.

I have been home sick for a week
Steadily getting worse and zero energy
Coughing so hard it feels like my brain is
rattling in my skull
This is Covid.

I have been home, alone, for ten days

Feeling a bit better, but the loneliness is
tremendous
Fear, depression and anxiety are taking over
Things no one mentions, about Covid.

I have been home sick and alone for fourteen
days
Depression and dreams of death consume me
Have not touched another human in two weeks
Recovering from Covid.

I go back to work tomorrow after two weeks of
solitude
To be able to have face to face conversations
floods me with joy
Still experiencing symptoms although improving
daily, time for another test
Negative for Covid.

It has been one month since I tested negative
I would not wish that mental headspace on my
worst enemy
Still cannot take a deep breath, lungs are healing
slowly
Residual effects of Covid.

Questions For Him

Am I what he wants in a partner?
Am I loving him in the ways he needs?
Am I overstepping his boundaries?
Am I supportive and uplifting enough?

Does he feel like we're on track?
Does he consider me when making decisions?
Does he truly want to be a husband and father?
Does he have concerns he's not voicing?

Will he ever open up to me?
Will he ever put me first in his life?
Will he fight for me and our relationship?
Will he ever truly trust me?

Is he happy with our relationship?
Is he waiting for the "other shoe to drop"?
Is he needing something more or different from
me?
Is he satisfied with me as his girlfriend?

How do we move past our emotional deficits?
How do we continue moving forward?
How do we make more time for each other?
How do we more effectively communicate?

Ocean Therapy

Salty water scents
Cool breeze like a gentle kiss
Roaring waves crashing

Sand beneath bare feet
Sea consuming fears and doubts
Warmth of summer sun

Sitting for hours
Watching, listening, breathing
Total soul repair

Oh, Sweet Nephew

Becoming your auntie has brought me great
delight
You bring life much laughter and light
I never knew a love like this until you
You filled a piece of my soul with the precious
things you do
Your cooing, giggles and learning to sit
Still can't believe I'm missing all of it
It makes my heart ache, being so far away
Until we're together, I'll call you every day
We'll send pictures and videos again and again
Together in two months if we can wait until then
I'll video-chat with you from afar
So that daily you know how adored you are
You are a precious gift from above
I'll never stop showing you enormous amounts
of love
Don't you ever forget, dear sweet nephew
My whole world is brighter because of you

Wedding Day Dreams

As a little girl, I dreamt of my wedding day
Being the bride in a beautiful white dress
Using dandelions as a bouquet and a pillowcase
as a veil
Getting married on the playground

As a teenager, I dreamt of my wedding day
Playing M.A.S.H. to pick bridesmaid dress
colors
Deciding between roses or lilies; in a church or
at the beach
Pondering if my boyfriend is "the one"

As a young adult, I dreamt of my wedding day
Trying to find the man of my dreams, the perfect
husband
Picking bridesmaids from childhood friends to
co-workers and roommates
Checking out which engagement ring styles suit
me best

As a woman in her twenties, I dreamt of my
wedding day
Fearing it's too late or I missed my chance
Hoping that the man of my dreams is still out
there, somewhere
Dating men I should not have trying to find him

As a woman in my thirties, I still dream of my
wedding day
Wanting a small, intimate ceremony instead of a
big white wedding
Praying for my future husband, his life, his
health
Wondering if I finally found the one I've been
waiting for

All my life I envisioned my wedding day
Now, I dream of marriage
Gaining a partner to build a life with
Creating a loving home and nurturing a family

Tired

Tired of being caught in the middle
Hardly ever sleeping
Tired of being second choice
And of the constant weeping
Tired of being overwhelmed
Being badly treated
Tired of lies and gossip
Tired of feeling so defeated
Tired of the backstabbing
The slander and the scandal
Tired of the ups and downs
And the things that you can't handle

The Man I Prayed For

For years, I anxiously awaited the arrival of my
perfect match
Growing more impatient with every failed
relationship
Wondering when I would find him
Praying, hoping and wishing that he would be
Kind and compassionate with an aptitude for
helping people
Loyal and honest with non-judgmental, listening
ears
Adventurous and courageous with stories of
experiences and travels
Humorous and charismatic with an infectious
laugh and smile
Intelligent and curious with a hobby he'll teach
me about
Humble and thoughtful with a dignified
demeanor
Tall and handsome with strong hands and arms
to hold me

Family oriented and a leader with vision for the
future
Protective and resilient with a dependable and
assertive nature
Hardworking and providing with goals and
ambition
Finally, I found a man with all these traits
He is a wonderful partner and our future
together looks bright
Every morning I wake up thanking God for this
man
Every night I go to bed wondering how I got so
lucky

You Burned That Bridge

This is an enormous betrayal
All these lies and slander
The backstabbing, the selfishness
Trust is forever broken
Belittling me out of envy
Slinging disrespectful insults

There will be no stooping to your level
I will not escalate the issues
On high alert to your rumormongering
Discouraging the toxicity
Practicing dignity and self-restraint
Though, I will not ignore the gossip

Everyone will see the truth
Support surrounds me in trusted alliances
Providing uplifting words of encouragement
Reinforcing my self-esteem
Protecting myself with knowledge
Karma has a lot to offer you, enjoy

Precious Family Time

Whimpers from the baby wake me up
Eyes open to see my handsome husband,
sleeping soundly
I get up, put on my robe and slippers and walk
into the nursery
Stuffed cars and trucks spin on the mobile above
the crib
I look down to see a perfect baby boy, grinning
up at me
Kissing his chubby cheeks as I pick him up
Walk back, crawl into bed as I snuggle him
closely
My husband stirs and awakens to me nursing our
baby
He kisses my forehead and gently rubs the
baby's head
Smiling, lovingly at each other as we hear little
feet patter down the hallway
Our beautiful three year old daughter enters and
asks for help onto our bed
My husband lifts her up, kisses her and cozies
her between us

Looking at my family, I cannot help but express
my love to them
A perfect moment with my handsome husband,
gorgeous daughter and adorable son
Then, I awaken, alone
That beautiful family was a dream
Perfect moment taken away in an instant
Heartbroken, tears fill my eyes wishing that was
my reality

Be My Escape

Overwhelmed by feelings
Desperately needing a release
Turning to art for comfort
Having creativity flowing
Helps to calm spirit, mind, body, soul

Music to soothe my spirit
Melodies to elevate me
Harmonies to guide me on a journey
Bass lines to ground me
Drums to drown out sorrows

Movies to occupy my mind
Comedies to make me laugh
Musicals to inspire my voice
Action sequences to excite me
Fantasy worlds to transport me

Painting to relax my body
Easels to provide me balance
Lines to give me structure
Mixing colors to create beauty from chaos
Shading to focus my thoughts

Writing to expose my soul

Poetry to process emotions
Stories to vacation to another place
Songs to release intense sentiments
Memoirs to demonstrate growth

Immersing myself in creative outlets
If only for an hour or two
Awakens my soul, rejuvenated and refreshed
Creativity is therapy
Art is my escape

Beloved Grandparents

TGrandfather, the patriarch of our family
Veteran of the United States Air Force
Storyteller of days gone by
Minister of God's word
Consumer of a spoonful of peanut butter
Watcher of John Wayne movies and sports
Encourager of hopes and dreams
Maker of the best homemade ice cream and hot
chocolate
Creator of beautiful cradles where his
grandchildren slept
Player of Solitaire, Pinochle and Tripoli

Grandmother, the matriarch of our family
Hostess of elegant and extravagant tea parties
Singer of lullabies and hymns
Photographer of countless memories placed into
scrapbooks
Listener of problems while sitting in a rocking
chair on the porch
Creator of family traditions and beautiful
greeting cards

Genealogist of the family and the history that
lies therein
Baker of homemade scones, pies, cookies and
cakes
Leader of prayers and devotions
Cook of family recipes handed down through
generations

This is how I choose to think about my
grandparents
The thoughtful, caring and generous leaders of
our family
Demonstrating the kind of relationship everyone
should aspire to have
Ministering to people from all walks of life

This is how I choose to remember my
grandparents
As they were, before Covid wreaked havoc on
their minds
Desperately hoping their memories return
Praying for complete healing and restoration

You Are Enough

Pessimistic remarks made loudly enough to hear
Too tall or too short; too fat or too thin
Society says you're supposed to look a certain
way
Model yourself after celebrities; make
improvements
Change your hair; lose weight; buy different
clothes
Not allowed to be satisfied with who they are

Appreciate all your body can do
Appearance does not equal self-worth
Love your body, just as it is
Radiate beauty from within
Feel satisfied with your choices
Do your best, you are enough

Surprise On A Sunday

To say he's hardworking is an understatement
A minimum of six days a week
Not at all faulting him for this trait
Just wishing we could spend more time together
Those concerns were voiced a few days back
Hearing me and taking action
A text and said he'll be over soon
Imagine my surprise, because he works
Saturdays
Spending the day in each other's company
Movies, snacks and enjoying time together
Ending our day at my dad's for family dinner
Even though he has a hard time expressing his
feelings
Actions speak louder than words
He'll never know how much that day meant to
me
Reassurance given by putting me first
Shows me how much I mean to him

You Thought You Could Break Me

After years of manipulation,
Lies, gossip, dragging my name through the
mud...
My eyes were finally opened.
She no longer deserved to be part of my life.
Unacceptable to her that I removed myself as
her minion,
The retaliation that resulted was dreadful.
Irreparable damages to my career, family, mental
health and finances
All collapsed at once with her final act.
Removing me from my extended family and
second home,
I was refused the chance to even advocate for
myself.
Experiencing emotional distress and with no
choice in the matter,
I attempt to regain my dignity with grace and
class.
Now gone, the effects of her reign remain...
But her feeble attempts did not destroy me.

Suffering through adversity only made me more
determined.
I will persevere.

I Am

A lioness, protective and bold
A whale, playful and wise
A bear, responsible and devoted
An elephant, compassionate and gentle

The sun, bright and resilient
The moon, passionate and loyal
The stars, artistic and sincere
The planets, proud and adventurous

A mountain, grounded and powerful
A forest, wild and spiritual
A river, open and persistent
An ocean, strong and fierce

The wind, lively and driven
The rain, practical and dependable
The snow, patient and authentic
The storm, sassy and loud

Polycystic Ovarian Syndrome

A diagnosis five years ago changed my life
forever
Polycystic Ovarian Syndrome
Rapid weight gain and difficulty losing it
Hair will grow in places it isn't meant to
Acne I had as a teenager is back
Handfuls of hair will fall from my head
Add depression, anxiety and insomnia
Ovarian cysts, insulin resistance, and mood
swings
Pelvic pain, possible boils and skin tags
Oh, I forgot to mention…..INFERTILITY
That one word, destroyed me
My body can't do what it's biologically
programmed to?
How did I get this? There's no clear cut answer
Could be environmental; could be genetic
How do we fix it? There's no cure
We treat the symptoms with medication
Meds, check. Diet, check. Exercise, check.
Nothing is working; all my symptoms remain

Change doctors, same treatment plan with
different medicine
I'll try anything to not feel like this anymore
Even meds administered through injections
No change, maybe another doctor?
Five in total and finally a glimmer of hope
New OBGYN has a plan and is confident
Realized dreams cover her walls with pictures
Miracle babies with grateful parents;
I could really get pregnant and be a mom?
When I'm ready, we'll begin treatments
For now, I'm preparing my body for that time
My greatest desire is to be a mother
What was once filled with sorrow;
Now is flooded with hope

Bringing It To A Close

These last few weeks have been challenging and emotional
Writing as an outlet to address those feelings
Expressing vulnerability in words
Doubts entering my mind
Will anyone relate to these struggles
Continuing to write, to refine, to adapt
Stronger now, feeling brave
Healthier headspace and capable of growth
Knowing I did my best
Prepared to face what comes next

www.ingramcontent.com/pod-product-compliance
Lightning Source LLC
La Vergne TN
LVHW021339200726
843509LV00014B/2576